Animal Attack and Defense

VENOM, POISON, AND ELECTRICITY

Kimberley Jane Pryor

Marshall Cavendish
Benchmark

New York

First published in 2008 by
MACMILLAN EDUCATION AUSTRALIA PTY LTD
15–19 Claremont Street, South Yarra 3141

Visit our website at www.macmillan.com.au or go directly to www.macmillanlibrary.com.au

Associated companies and representatives throughout the world.

Library of Congress Cataloging-in-Publication Data

Pryor, Kimberley Jane.
    Venom, poison, and electricity / by Kimberley Jane Pryor.
        p. cm. – (Animal attack and defense)
    Includes index.
    Summary: "Discusses how animals use venom, poison, and electricity to protect themselves from predators
or to catch prey"–Provided by publisher.
    ISBN 978-0-7614-4422-0
    1. Poisonous animals–Juvenile literature. 2. Electric fishes–Juvenile literature. I. Title.
    QL100.P79 2009
591.6'5–dc22
                                                                                    2009004994

Edited by Julia Carlomagno
Text and cover design by Ben Galpin
Page layout by Domenic Lauricella
Photo research by Claire Armstrong and Legend Images

Printed in the United States

Acknowledgments
The author and the publisher are grateful to the following for permission to reproduce copyright material:

Cover and title page photo of a puff adder © Photolibrary/Tony Allen

Photos courtesy of: © Blickwinkel/Alamy/Photolibrary, **11**; © Wolfgang Pölzer/Alamy/Photolibrary, **28**; © Kathie
Atkinson/Auscape, **7**; © D Parer & E Parer-Cook/Auscape, **5**; © Getty Images/Altrendo Nature, **16**; © Getty
Images/David Doubilet/National Geographic, **14**; © Getty Images/Georgette Douwma, **18**; © Getty Images/
Michael & Patricia Fogden, **30** (right); © Getty Images/Frans Lemmens, **10**; © Getty Images/Piotr Naskrecki,
22; © Getty Images/Travel Ink, **8**; © Getty Images/David Wrobel, **12**, **13**, **29**; © Getty Images/Norbert Wu,
27; © Sharif El-Hamalawi/iStockphoto.com, **15**; © Jeridu/iStockphoto.com, **4**; © Photolibrary/Tony Allen, **30**
(left); Photolibrary/Max Gibbs, **24**; Photolibrary/Zigmund Leszczynski, **21**; Photolibrary/Chris McLaughlin, **20**;
Photolibrary/Richard Nowitz/PRI, **26**; Photolibrary/William S Peckover, **19**; Photolibrary/Juan Manuel Renjifo,
23; Photolibrary/Superstock Inc, **6**; Photolibrary/James Urbach, **17**; Photos.com, **9**; © David Snyder, **25**.

For Nick, Ashley, and Thomas

1 3 5 6 4 2

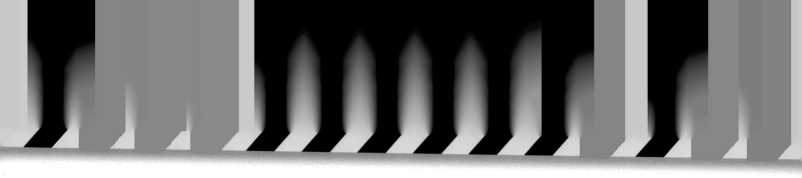

Glossary Word

When a word is printed in **bold**, you can look up its meaning in the glossary on page 31.

Types of Venom

Different types of venom have different effects on victims. Venom can be injected into a victim by fangs, teeth, stings, spines, or claws. Some types of venom damage a victim's brain and nervous system. The victim becomes **paralyzed** and stops breathing. Some types of venom damage the heart and blood vessels, and some cause **allergic reactions**.

Centipedes use claws near their heads to inject venom into their victims.

> A **venom** is a poison that some animals have. It causes illness or death if it is injected into other animals.

A male platypus can stab predators with the sharp, venomous spurs on his back legs.

How Venom Protects Animals

Venomous animals have very good chances of surviving if attacked. Even before venom takes effect, the pain of a bite or sting is enough to make most **predators** back off. If a predator survives, it will remember the pain and illness caused by the venom for a long time. It will think carefully before attacking that type of animal, or entering its **habitat** again.

5

Frightening Fangs.........

Black Mambas

Vital Statistics

- **Length:** 7.9 to 14.1 feet (2.4 to 4.3 meters)
- **Habitat:** rocky open country
- **Distribution:** Africa
- **Predators:** none known

A Black Mamba's Fangs

The fangs of a black mamba deliver venom that acts on a victim's nerves and heart. The venom can kill an adult human in as little as twenty minutes.

Black mambas are among Africa's most feared snakes. Before **antivenom** was available, a bite from a black mamba was always deadly to humans.

A black mamba lifts the front third of its body off the ground when it is threatened. It flattens its neck and hisses loudly, then displays its fearsome fangs and inky black mouth. If a predator does not leave, a black mamba **strikes** several times. It injects powerful, fast-acting venom with every strike.

A black mamba injects venom through fangs in the front of its upper jaw.

Some venomous animals deliver their venom through long, sharp, hollow, or grooved fangs.

A Sydney funnel-web spider rears up and releases venom onto its fangs if it feels threatened.

Vital Statistics

- **Length:** 0.6 to 1.4 inches (1.5 to 3.5 centimeters)
- **Habitat:** moist, sheltered places
- **Distribution:** Australia
- **Predators:** lizards and birds

Sydney Funnel-Web Spiders

Sydney funnel-web spiders are among the world's deadliest spiders. The male funnel-web delivers powerful venom through his huge fangs.

Sydney funnel-web spiders are extremely aggressive if they feel threatened. A male funnel-web is much more dangerous than a female. He rears up and moves his fangs into the striking position if threatened. Then he strikes downward at lightning speed.

A Sydney Funnel-Web Spider's Fangs

The fangs of a Sydney funnel-web spider deliver venom that affects a victim's nerves. There have been fourteen recorded deaths from Sydney funnel-web spider bites.

A Blue-Ringed Octopus's Bite

The bite of a blue-ringed octopus releases venom that acts on a victim's nerves. A human may die in as little as ninety minutes from a blue-ringed octopus's bite.

Blue-Ringed Octopuses

Blue-ringed octopuses are stunning but dangerous sea creatures. Their venomous bite are some of the deadliest bites known.

A blue-ringed octopus hides in small crevices in rock pools. If it feels threatened, it displays its bright blue rings as a warning sign. Then it bites. The bite does not hurt very much, but the venom goes to work immediately. The victim becomes paralyzed and stops breathing.

The rings on a blue-ringed octopus glow brightly to warn predators that the octopus might bite.

Some venomous animals inject venom into victims with their powerful bites.

A Gila monster can give a quick but painful venomous bite.

Gila Monsters

Gila monsters are one of only two kinds of venomous lizards in the world. When a Gila monster bites, it holds on tightly to its victim and chews venom into the wound.

A Gila monster is a shy lizard that is rarely seen. However, when it is threatened by a predator, it opens its mouth and hisses loudly. If this warning is ignored, it latches onto the predator and chews. Venom from **glands** in its lower jaw flows through its grooved teeth and into the wound.

Vital Statistics

- **Length:** 2 ft (60 cm)
- **Habitat:** deserts
- **Distribution:** North America
- **Predators:** cats and dogs

A Gila Monster's Bite

A Gila monster's bite releases venom that acts on a victim's nerves. The bite is painful to humans, but the venom rarely causes death.

Scorpions

A Scorpion's Sting

A scorpion's sting delivers venom that acts on a victim's nerves. Venom from some types of scorpions is deadly to humans.

S corpions are often feared by campers, who do not want to find one in their shoes. A scorpion defends itself with a venomous sting at the tip of its tail.

When attacked, a scorpion holds the predator with its **pincers** and stings over and over again. It thrusts its tail over its body and pushes the sharp, hollow sting into the victim's flesh. With each sting, it releases a dose of venom.

The fat-tailed scorpion has enough venom to kill an adult human.

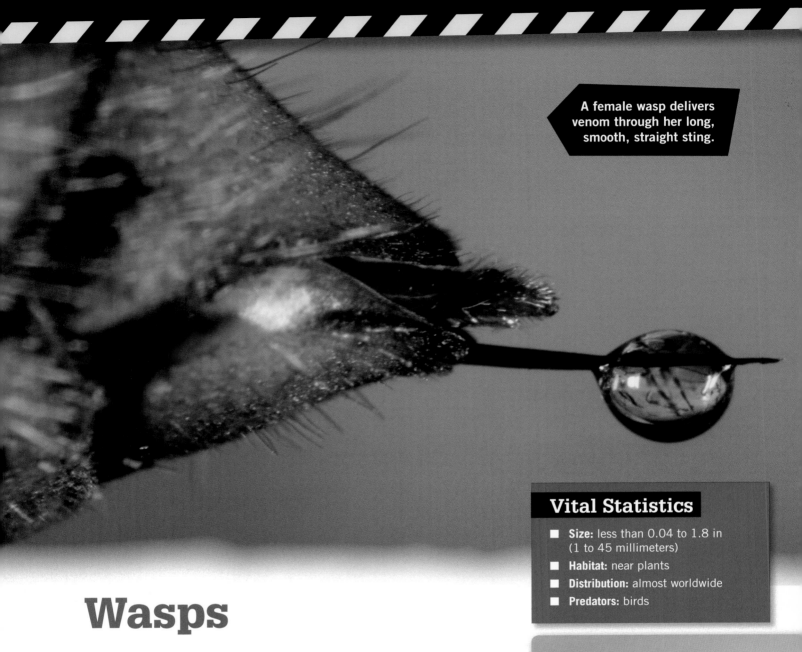

Many small animals are highly venomous. Scorpions and wasps deliver venom through stings.

A female wasp delivers venom through her long, smooth, straight sting.

Vital Statistics

- **Size:** less than 0.04 to 1.8 in (1 to 45 millimeters)
- **Habitat:** near plants
- **Distribution:** almost worldwide
- **Predators:** birds

Wasps

Some wasps are aggressive insects. A female wasp can sting repeatedly with the venomous sting on the end of her **abdomen**.

When a wasp nest is under threat, female wasps fly out and sting the **intruder**. As soon as the sharp stings pierce the intruder's skin, venom is pumped into the wound. A wasp can sting over and over again.

A Wasp's Sting

A wasp's sting delivers venom that can cause severe allergic reactions. Humans who are allergic to wasp stings often die if they do not receive medical attention immediately.

Box Jellyfish

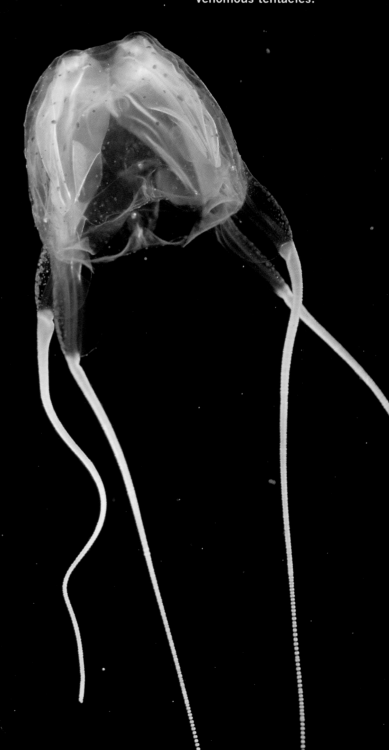

A box jellyfish has four bundles of long, venomous tentacles.

Box jellyfish are among the most dangerous animals in the world. Victims of their venomous stings often need medical attention immediately after being stung in order to survive.

A box jellyfish trails its tentacles behind as it swims. The tentacles are covered in stinging cells. When an animal brushes against them, each stinging cell that has been touched fires a hollow thread. Venom flows through the hollow threads and into the animal.

Vital Statistics

- **Length:** 9.8 ft (3 m)
- **Habitat:** river mouths
- **Distribution:** Indian and Pacific oceans
- **Predators:** turtles

A Box Jellyfish's Tentacles

The venom from a box jellyfish's stinging tentacles acts on a victim's nerves, heart, and skin. It can kill an adult human in as little as three minutes.

Cone Shells

Pretty cone shells look harmless enough. However, they have a secret weapon. They can shoot out venomous, barbed darts.

Cone shells are small animals that move slowly along the ocean floor. When a cone shell is attacked, it aims a long, flexible tube at the predator. Then, before the predator can flee, it fires a venomous barbed dart.

Vital Statistics

- **Length:** 0.4 to 4.7 in (1 to 12 cm)
- **Habitat:** coral reefs
- **Distribution:** Indian and Pacific oceans
- **Predators:** turtles

A Cone Shell's Dart

A cone shell's dart delivers venom that acts on a victim's nerves. The venom may cause the victim to stop breathing, and then die.

A cone shell fires a dart containing venom at predators.

A reef stonefish has 13 spines to inject venom into victims.

Vital Statistics

- **Length:** 1.1 ft (35 cm)
- **Habitat:** coral reefs
- **Distribution:** Indian and Pacific oceans
- **Predators:** sharks and rays

A Reef Stonefish's Spines

The spines of a reef stonefish inject venom that acts on a victim's nerves, heart, and blood cells. It can be deadly to humans.

Reef Stonefish

Reef stonefish are the most dangerous venomous fish in the world. They inject venom into their victims through spines that sit along their backs.

A reef stonefish lies very still among rocks or coral on the ocean floor. If it is stepped on, a reef stonefish's sharp spines puncture the victim's foot. The pressure of the foot causes venom to flow up the spines and into the puncture wound. The venom can be deadly to humans.

Stingrays can defend themselves against predators with their needle-sharp venomous spines.

Stingrays

Stingrays have a powerful defense, although they are not aggressive animals. Each stingray has one or more long, venomous spines on its whiplike tail.

A stingray spends a lot of time lying on the ocean floor, partly covered by sand. If it is attacked by a predator, a stingray flips up its tail and drives its venomous spines deep into the predator's flesh. The spines often break off in the wound, causing severe pain and swelling.

Vital Statistics

- **Length:** up to 14.1 ft (4.3 m)
- **Habitat:** ocean floor
- **Distribution:** warm coastal waters worldwide
- **Predators:** sharks

A Stingray's Spines

A stingray's spines inject venom that acts on a victim's nerves and body tissues. The venom is usually not deadly, but the injury from the **serrated** spines can be.

Saddleback Caterpillars

Vital Statistics

- **Length:** 1 in (25 mm)
- **Habitat:** basswood, chestnut, cherry, plum, and oak trees
- **Distribution:** North America
- **Predators:** birds

A Saddleback Caterpillar's Spines

The venomous spines of a saddleback caterpillar cause pain, redness, and swelling. They may cause severe allergic reactions in some people.

Saddleback caterpillars are animals to stay away from! They have four fleshy horns covered with venomous spines, and clusters of venomous spines along their sides.

A saddleback caterpillar crawls over plants, feasting on tasty leaves. If it is touched, a saddleback caterpillar's hollow spines break and release venom onto a victim's skin. If it is pressed more forcefully, a saddleback caterpillar's spines puncture the victim's skin and release venom into the puncture wounds.

A saddleback caterpillar's bold pattern warns that its venomous spines are dangerous.

Some of the most beautiful caterpillars are also the most dangerous. They have **clusters** of sharp, venomous spines.

An Io moth caterpillar can defend itself from predators with its venomous spines.

Io Moth Caterpillars

Stunning Io moth caterpillars are dangerous insects. They are covered in clusters of venomous green spines.

Io moth caterpillars travel together in long trains over plants. A person who brushes against an Io moth caterpillar's venomous spines feels a stinging or burning sensation. The effect is worse if the spines puncture the skin and release venom into the puncture wound.

Vital Statistics

- **Length:** 2 to 3.1 in (5 to 8 cm)
- **Habitat:** corn, roses, willow, linden, elm, oak, locust, apple, beech, ash, currant, and clover plants
- **Distribution:** North America
- **Predators:** birds

An Io Moth Caterpillar's Spines

The venomous spines of an Io moth caterpillar cause a very painful skin rash. They may cause severe allergic reactions in some people.

Types of Poison

Different types of poison act on victims in different ways. Poison gets into a victim's body when the victim touches or eats a poisonous animal. Some types of poison act on the nerves, and cause a victim to become paralyzed and stop breathing. Some types of poison act on the heart and blood vessels.

Humpback snapper become poisonous if they eat certain foods.

A poison is a substance that can cause illness or death if it is touched, breathed in, or swallowed.

A variable pitohui is a bird with poisonous skin and poisonous feathers.

How Poisons Protect Animals

Poisons protect animals from being eaten by predators. Many poisonous animals have bright warning colors that give predators a clear message: "Don't touch me, I'm poisonous!" If predators ignore the message, they may be poisoned and die. If they touch or try to eat a poisonous animal and survive, they will remember not to touch this kind of animal in the future.

Vital Statistics

- **Length:** 1 in to 2 ft (2.5 to 61 cm)
- **Habitat:** river mouths and coastal waters
- **Distribution:** warm waters worldwide
- **Predators:** sharks

A Puffer Fish's Poison

A puffer fish's poison acts on a victim's nerves. Some people eat Japanese puffer fish, even though they risk being poisoned. Every year, many people die from eating puffer fish.

Puffer Fish

Puffer fish contain a deadly poison in their livers, ovaries, intestines, and skins. One puffer fish has enough poison to kill thirty adults.

A puffer fish is an easy target for a predator because it swims very slowly. When it is threatened, it gulps down water or air to make itself look bigger. A predator that attacks a puffer fish is in for a surprise. Not only does a puffer fish **inflate** itself, but the poison gives it a foul taste.

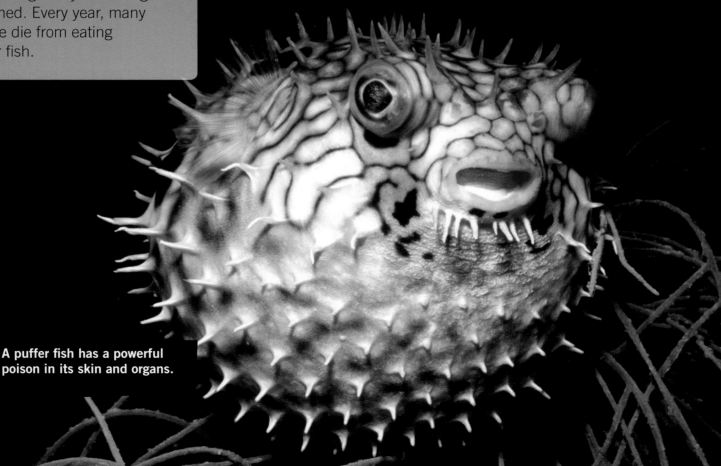

A puffer fish has a powerful poison in its skin and organs.

A California newt releases powerful poison through its skin if it is attacked.

California Newts

Cal"ifornia newts can release a deadly poison from glands in their skins. The poison can easily kill a human.

A California newt looks tasty to predators. However, it is not safe to eat. If a California newt is threatened, it displays its orange belly to predators as a warning. If a predator attacks, a California newt releases poison through its warty skin.

Vital Statistics

- **Length:** 5.9 in (15 cm)
- **Habitat:** near streams and ponds
- **Distribution:** North America
- **Predators:** snakes

A California Newt's Poison

A California newt's poison acts on a victim's nerves. It can kill most animals, including humans.

Cane Toads

Vital Statistics

- **Length:** 3.9 to 5.9 in (10 to 15 cm)
- **Habitat:** most habitats with water
- **Distribution:** Central and South America, the Philippines, and Australia
- **Predators:** lizards, snakes, rats, and birds

Cane toads are pests that have been brought into many countries. A cane toad's poison can kill a native animal or a pet in as little as fifteen minutes.

When a cane toad is attacked by a predator, it turns to the side so that its poison glands are facing the attacker. A milky, poisonous fluid oozes out of the poison glands. A cane toad can squirt the poisonous fluid up to 3.3 feet (1 meter) away.

A Cane Toad's Poison

A cane toad's poison affects a victim's heart. It also causes severe pain if it gets into the eyes or mouth.

A cane toad has a large poison gland on each shoulder.

The yellow skin of golden poison frogs warns of their deadly poison.

Golden Poison Frogs

Vital Statistics

- **Length:** 2 in (5 cm)
- **Habitat:** rain forests
- **Distribution:** South America
- **Predators:** snakes

Tiny golden poison frogs are the most poisonous frogs in the world. Their bodies contain enough poison to kill ten adult humans.

A golden poison frog lives in damp leaf litter on the rain forest floor. It releases poison through its skin when threatened. A predator that tries to eat a golden poison frog will quickly spit it out because of the foul taste. However, the predator will die if the poison gets into a cut in its mouth.

A Golden Poison Frog's Poison

A golden poison frog's poison acts on a victim's nerves and heart. It is one of the most powerful natural poisons in the world.

23

The smallmouth electric catfish can produce powerful electric shocks.

Types of Electricity

Different types of fish produce electric shocks from different types of **electric organs**. An electric eel produces powerful electric shocks from electric organs in its tail. An electric catfish produces electricity from a jellolike electric organ beneath its skin. An electric ray has a large, jelly-bean-shaped electric organ on either side of its head. It can produce electric shocks measuring between 8 and 220 volts.

How Electricity Protects Animals

Electricity protects animals from being eaten by predators. An electric shock can be deadly or very unpleasant to a predator. A predator that has been shocked will most likely stay away from the area in future.

Some fish can deliver electric shocks at will to defend themselves or their **territory**. The bigger the fish, the bigger the electric shock.

A stargazer produces an electric shock from an organ in a pouch behind its eyes.

Severe Shocks.........

An electric eel's electric organs can deliver severe electric shocks.

Vital Statistics

- **Length:** 8.2 ft (2.5 m)
- **Habitat:** slow-moving freshwater
- **Distribution:** South America
- **Predators:** none known

An Electric Eel's Electric Shock

An electric eel's electric shock can measure up to 650 volts. Repeated electric shocks may kill a human.

Electric Eels

Electric eels are the most dangerous electric fish. They can deliver electric shocks powerful enough to knock horses off their feet.

Electric eels lurk in murky streams and ponds. They have large electric organs, which take up four-fifths of their bodies. Electric eels deliver powerful electric shocks if touched or stepped on. They also use electricity to **navigate**, to communicate, and to stun or kill **prey**.

Electric Catfish

The electric catfish is an aggressive fish. It uses electric shocks to defend its territory against intruders.

The electric catfish hides during the day and hunts for fish at night. Its electric organ forms a layer directly under its skin. If an intruder enters its territory, it delivers a series of powerful electric shocks. The electric catfish also uses electricity to capture prey.

Vital Statistics

- **Length:** 3.9 ft (1.2 m)
- **Habitat:** dark, still freshwater
- **Distribution:** Africa
- **Predators:** none known

An Electric Catfish's Electric Shock

An electric catfish's electric shock can measure up to 350 volts. It feels very unpleasant, but is not deadly to humans.

An electric catfish defends its territory by delivering electric shocks.

Numbfish can keep well-hidden, and zap intruders with a sudden jolt of electricity.

Vital Statistics

- **Length:** 2 ft (60 cm)
- **Habitat:** sandy and muddy ocean floor
- **Distribution:** Australia
- **Predators:** none known

A Numbfish's Electric Shock

A numbfish's electric shock can cause a human's muscles to cramp severely. However, the shock is not deadly to humans.

Numbfish

Numbfish are slow-moving rays that pack a powerful punch. They defend themselves by stunning predators with electricity.

A numbfish buries itself in sand or mud so that only its eyes and nostrils can be seen. It sometimes leaves a round pattern in the sand or mud above its body. It has a pair of jelly-bean-shaped electric organs in its head. If it is stepped on, a numbfish may deliver a powerful electric shock.

Pacific Electric Rays

Pacific electric rays are sometimes aggressive when they are disturbed. They give painful electric shocks when touched.

During the day, a Pacific electric ray rests on sandy ocean floors near rocky reefs and seaweed beds. It has a pair of jelly-bean-shaped electric organs in its head. If it is touched or stepped on, it may become aggressive and give a painful electric shock.

A Pacific Electric Ray's Electric Shock

A Pacific electric ray's electric shock can measure up to 50 volts. It is painful and teaches predators to stay away.

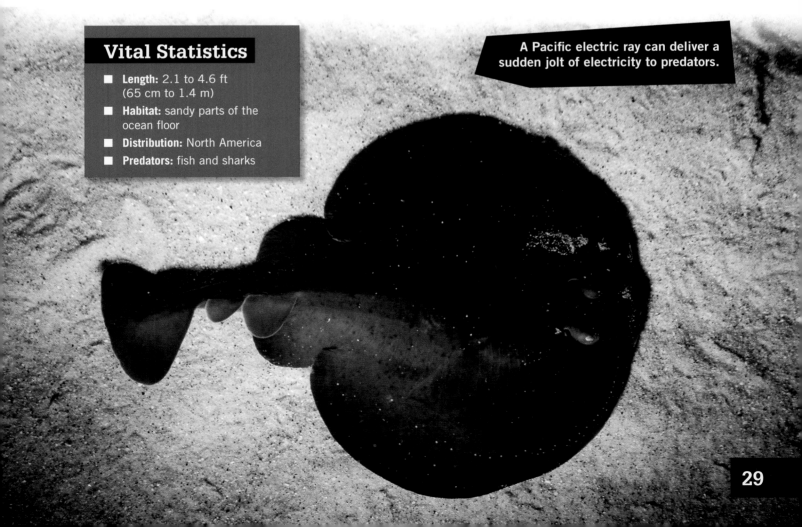

Vital Statistics

- **Length:** 2.1 to 4.6 ft (65 cm to 1.4 m)
- **Habitat:** sandy parts of the ocean floor
- **Distribution:** North America
- **Predators:** fish and sharks

A Pacific electric ray can deliver a sudden jolt of electricity to predators.

Double Defenses

Many animals have not just one, but two ways
to defend themselves from predators.

Puff Adders

Puff adders are common, yet very dangerous,
snakes. They use venom and camouflage to
defend themselves from predators.

Vital Statistics

- **Length:** 3.3 to 4.9 ft (1 to 1.5 m)
- **Habitat:** forests, grasslands, and swamps
- **Distribution:** Africa and Arabia
- **Predators:** other snakes, birds of prey,
  and warthogs

A Puff Adder's Venom

A puff adder uses venom to defend itself.
It does not flee from predators. Instead,
a puff adder puffs itself up and hisses in
warning. If the warning does not make
the predator back away, the puff adder
strikes with incredible force and speed.
It sinks its long, curved fangs into the
victim and injects its deadly venom.

A Puff Adder's Camouflage

A puff adder relies on its excellent
camouflage for protection. Its body is
yellow-brown to light brown, with dark
bars and thin yellow v-shaped bars.

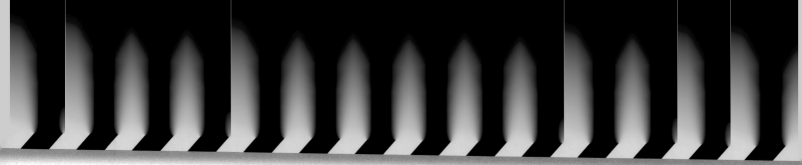

abdomen	the last section of the body of some invertebrates
allergic reactions	negative reactions in the body to some substances
antivenom	a treatment given to fight the effects of venom
clusters	groups
electric organs	parts of an animal's body which produce electricity
glands	groups of cells in the body that make and release substances, such as poison and venom
habitat	an area where animals live, feed, and breed
inflate	expand
intruder	unwelcome stranger
navigate	find one's way
paralyzed	unable to move
pincers	claws
predators	animals that hunt and kill other animals for food
prey	animals that are hunted and caught for food by other animals
serrated	having sharp notches along the edge
strikes	lunges forward and bites
territory	an area occupied by an animal, or group of animals
venom	a type of poison, made by an animal
venomous	poisonous